how to make
easy fudge

Beth Klosterboer

Meaghan Mountford

welcome

Step inside our world of fudge! Our goal is to share easy fudge recipes so you can make delicious homemade candy for every occasion.

With just a few ingredients and a few minutes in the kitchen, you'll create every flavor imaginable. We'll help you each step of the way with foolproof tips and tricks.

Each of these easy fudge recipes was originally created for our website, HowToMakeEasyFudge.com We compiled some of our most popular recipes to share with you in this book.
You can see more recipes and view all our video tutorials on the website.

Beth & Meaghan

copyright © 2020
photography © Beth Jackson Klosterboer
photography © Meaghan Mountford

ISBN: 9798681763284

All rights reserved. The reproduction, transmission or utilization of this work in whole or in part in any form by an electronic, mechanical or other means, now known and hereafter invented, including xerography, photocopying and recording, or in any information storage or retrieval system, is forbidden without the written permission of the publisher.
For permission please reach out to howtomakeeasyfudge@gmail.com.

table of contents

FUDGE BASICS   1

TRADITIONAL FUDGE   6

chocolate fudge
peanut butter fudge
chocolate peanut butter fudge
vanilla fudge
milk chocolate fudge
mint chocolate chip fudge
frosting fudge
marshmallow fudge
cookies and cream fudge
butterscotch fudge
chocolate coconut fudge
maple fudge

NUTTY & FRUITY FUDGE   19

rocky road fudge
butter pecan fudge
cashew butter fudge
maple walnut fudge
pumpkin fudge
lemon fudge
strawberry fudge
creamsicle fudge
key lime fudge
chocolate raspberry fudge

HOLIDAY FUDGE   30

countdown clock fudge
fudge hearts
strawberry frosting fudge
rainbow fudge
orange fudge carrots
red, white, and blue fudge
zombie fudge
fudge turkeys
peanut blossom fudge
peppermint bark fudge
eggnog fudge
chocolate peppermint fudge
fudge snowmen
fudge reindeer
Christmas fudge
"oh, fudge!" soap fudge

UNCONVENTIONAL FUDGE   47

caramel fudge
cake batter fudge
mermaid fudge
peanut butter cup fudge
cookie butter fudge
hazelnut spread fudge
buckeye fudge
cherry cola fudge
monster fudge
tiger butter fudge
cookie dough fudge
chocolate pretzel fudge
s'mores fudge
red velvet fudge
cotton candy fudge

BOOZY FUDGE

whiskey fudge
Irish creme fudge
vodka fudge
cinnamon whiskey fudge
gin fudge
tequila fudge
rum fudge

fudge basics

WHAT IS FUDGE?

Old fashioned fudge is *a soft candy made from sugar, milk or cream, butter, and flavorings*. The sugar and milk are heated to the "soft-ball stage" of candy-making on a candy thermometer to make a sugar syrup, then the butter, flavorings, and mix-ins like nuts are added. If this is all done properly you will make a smooth, creamy fudge. However, candy-making can be rather temperamental and tricky because the chemistry requires precision, and it takes a good bit of experience and practice to craft perfect old fashioned fudge.

But fear not! Every *quick and easy fudge recipe* you will find in this book can be made in minutes in the microwave or on the stove-top without the use of a candy thermometer. We have tricks to skip the tedious candy-making process by using alternative ingredients as shortcuts. Sweetened condensed milk, store-bought frosting, nut butter, and spreads work wonders here.

The delicious fudge recipes inside this book are more stable to prepare and easier to make for all skill levels. Some recipes have as few as *two* ingredients!

HOW TO PREPARE YOUR PAN. For many of the recipes, we suggest using an 8-inch square baking pan (for thicker fudge) or a 9-inch pan (for thinner fudge). You may even use an 8-inch by 4-inch loaf pan to make fudge slices instead of squares. You can use glass, ceramic, or metal pans. We recommend that no matter what type of pan you use that you butter or spray the pan or line it with non-stick aluminum foil. If you prefer, you can line your pan with regular tin foil or parchment paper that has been lightly sprayed with non-stick baking spray.

MAKE FUDGE WITH SWEETENED CONDENSED MILK. Sweetened condensed milk, which is essentially the sugar syrup part of fudge-making, is a great ingredient for making quick and easy fudge! You simply need to heat the sweetened condensed milk with chocolate chips on the stove-top or in the microwave, and add any flavoring or mix-ins you like to make delicious fudge.

Sweetened condensed milk is milk that has been pasteurized and condensed (cooked to remove most of the water) and sweetened with sugar. By using it you can essentially skip the fudge-making step of boiling sugar and dairy (milk, cream, or butter). The sugar also helps thicken and prolong the shelf life of the milk. Purchase 14-ounce cans from the grocery store and be sure to buy the right cans! **You CANNOT substitute evaporated milk.**

MAKE FUDGE WITH FROSTING, FRUIT CURD, JAM, NUT BUTTER, and MORE!
In this book, you will find many easy fudge recipes that use ingredients like lemon curd (pictured to the right), strawberry sauce, cashew butter, chocolate hazelnut spread, cookie butter, frosting, and more. Each of these delicious homemade candies is made using just two to four ingredients without the use of a candy thermometer.

MAKE FUDGE IN THE MICROWAVE. Many of our easy fudge recipes call for melting chocolate with sweetened condensed milk or any of the other items listed above. All of our instructions call for using the microwave at 70% power for 90-120 seconds to melt the chocolate and allowing the bowl to rest in the microwave for a few minutes to allow the heat to evenly distribute and for the chocolate to melt completely. If you prefer you can use the stovetop instead.

HOW TO MAKE FUDGE ON THE STOVE-TOP. Combine your chocolate and sweetened condensed milk in a medium saucepan. Set on the stovetop over **low** heat. Heat, stirring occasionally, until about 75% of the chocolate has melted. Remove from the heat and stir until smooth and creamy. If all the chocolate will not melt, allow the pan to sit for a few minutes, allowing the residual heat from the melted chocolate to melt the remaining solid chocolate, then stir again. If needed you can heat for another minute or so.

HOW TO MAKE FUDGE USING A DOUBLE BOILER: Alternatively, you may combine the chocolate and sweetened condensed milk in a heat-safe bowl and rest over a saucepan of simmering water and stir until melted. Just be sure the bottom of the bowl doesn't touch the water! This is a very safe way to melt the chocolate but we still recommend taking the chocolate off the heat once 75% of it is melted and stir until completely melted.

CHOCOLATE

It is very important that you use chocolate that you like to eat! A bad tasting or bland tasting chocolate isn't going to make great fudge. If you like a particular brand of chocolate right out of the package then it will taste good in fudge. Don't use a chocolate you don't like hoping it will taste better as fudge. It won't!

TYPES OF CHOCOLATE TO USE TO MAKE FUDGE

Pure Dark Chocolate (semi-sweet or bittersweet) and Milk Chocolate contain cocoa butter and can be purchased in bars, blocks, wafers, pistoles (bean-shaped wafers), callets, and chips.

Any of these will work in our fudge recipes just be sure to finely chop your chocolate for even melting.

Milk chocolate sets softer than dark chocolate, so you cannot simply swap milk chocolate out for dark chocolate in a recipe. You'll need approximately 25% more milk chocolate than dark chocolate.

Pure White Chocolate contains cocoa butter while *white compound chocolate, also known as confectionery coating* (like Nestle® Premier White Morsels. or white Candy Melts), contains palm kernel oil (or another type of vegetable oil).

You can use either pure white chocolate or white compound chocolate to make fudge. White chocolate made with cocoa butter is softer than white chocolate made with vegetable oil, so you will need to add extra pure white chocolate to some recipes. Those quantities are listed in each recipe.

Be sure to always check the ingredients list on the package of your white chocolate. Some chips are pure white chocolate while others are compound chocolate.

Peanut Butter Chips, Butterscotch Chips, Salted Caramel Chips, and seasonal flavored chips can also be used to make easy fudge.

HOW LONG IT TAKES FOR FUDGE TO SET. Most of our easy fudge recipes call for the fudge to be refrigerated for 2 to 4 hours. Some fudges may be firm and ready to cut sooner, and others may take longer. The time it takes will depend on how hot the fudge was when poured into the pan, the temperature of your refrigerator, and the ingredients used. You can also simply cover your fudge and allow it to cool at room temperature for approximately 8 hours or overnight.

If you remove your fudge from the pan and it's too sticky to cut, chill it longer. One trick is to set the fudge upside down, so the bottom dries a bit before cutting.

HOW TO STORE FUDGE. Fudge will stay fresh for at least 2 weeks and up to 3 months depending on how it is stored. Plain fudge has the longest shelf life. Mix-ins such as cookies and nuts will shorten the lifespan and soften the fudge.

To store your fudge at room temperature, you may wrap your fudge in wax paper, tin foil, or plastic wrap then store it in an airtight container or a zip-top bag.

You can enhance the shelf life of your fudge by storing it in a metal tin. Packaging fudge in tins is also a great way to give it as a gift. You can line the tin with wax paper, parchment paper, or tin foil for easy removal or just simply stack the fudge in the tin.

To store your fudge in the refrigerator, package as suggested for room temperature then place in the refrigerator. Note that refrigerated fudge should be removed and kept in it's packaging for about an hour before unwrapping to avoid any condensation forming on the top of the fudge.

You can store fudge in the freezer for up to 3 months if it is wrapped properly. Wrap the fudge well in plastic wrap or wax paper then wrap it tightly in tin foil and place in a zip top bag or airtight container to avoid ice crystals forming on the top of your fudge. To thaw your frozen fudge, remove the wrapped fudge from the freezer and let it sit at room temperature for a couple of hours before unwrapping. This will keep your fudge from developing beads of condensation which will make the surface of your fudge sticky.

TROUBLESHOOTING

Even with the simplest of recipes, we all have those days where something goes wrong. Here are some fixes just in case you have any problems.

SOFT FUDGE THAT WON'T SET. Your fudge will be too soft if you do not use the correct amount or type of chocolate. Fudge with chocolate and sweetened condensed milk, frosting, or sauce will be too soft if you don't use enough chocolate. The ratio needs to be just right, so be sure to follow our instructions and use the chocolate that is called for in the recipe.

Another issue can be the consistency of the sweetened condensed milk. Store brands of sweetened condensed milk tend to be thinner and runnier than name brands, and they may produce softer fudge. We recommend you add additional chocolate if using thin condensed milk.

HOW TO FIX SOFT FUDGE. You can chill soft fudge overnight to firm up enough to cut it, but if it is just too soft to hold its shape, your only option is to reheat it until it completely melts then stir in some melted chocolate. Or you can just eat it with a spoon!

FIXING DRY FUDGE. It's very unusual for easy fudge to become dry and crumbly, however, if you add too much chocolate, it is possible for the fudge to be too firm or even too dry. As mentioned above, you can reheat the fudge until it melts, then stir in more of the thick liquid called for in the recipe.

FIXING GREASY FUDGE. With an easy fudge recipe, the cocoa butter can separate from the chocolate if it gets too hot. If you follow our instructions for heating your fudge, then you should not have any issues, but if you do overheat the fudge and it looks greasy, pour it into a clean bowl and let it rest for 15 minutes. Then stir the fudge, working the cocoa butter back into the fudge. This is important so that the fudge is creamy. If you simply wipe up the cocoa butter, your fudge may become dry.

If the fudge still looks greasy, pour it out onto a cool surface like a marble cutting board, a granite countertop, or a cookie sheet and spread it thin, then scrape it up into a ball. Repeat this process until it no longer looks greasy. The fudge will be quite thick, so you'll have to push it into the pan.

WHY IS MY BOOZY FUDGE TOO THICK? Often, boozy fudge is made by adding a small amount of alcohol to sweetened condensed milk and melted chocolate. However, the alcohol flavor is significantly reduced in those recipes. Therefore, to have a strong alcohol flavor, we combine a good amount of alcohol with melted chocolate and powdered sugar. Without the sweetened condensed milk, the melted chocolate can be finicky. To avoid having your chocolate seize (or harden too quickly), be sure to use ***room-temperature alcohol*** and do not overheat the chocolate.

traditional fudge flavors

dark chocolate fudge

Serves 16 | Prep 10 mins | Cook 1 1/2 mins

INGREDIENTS

12 ounces semi-sweet chocolate, finely chopped pieces or chips

14 ounces sweetened condensed milk

Optional ingredients:

1 teaspoon pure vanilla extract or vanilla bean paste

1 pinch salt

DIRECTIONS

1. Combine the semi-sweet chocolate and sweetened condensed milk in a microwave-safe bowl.
2. Heat at 70% power for 90 seconds.
3. Allow the bowl to rest in the warm microwave for 3 minutes.
4. Remove the bowl and stir the chocolate until melted.
5. If needed, heat for 15-second increments at 70% power, stirring after each, until melted.
6. If using, stir in the vanilla and salt.
7. Pour the fudge into a greased or lined 8-inch square pan and spread into an even layer.
8. Allow the fudge to cool at room temperature for about 8 hours or chill in the refrigerator until firm, about 3 hours.
9. Cut into 16 squares.

NOTES

You can pour the fudge into an 8-inch by 4-inch loaf pan and cut it into slices for a different look.

peanut butter fudge

Serves 24 | Prep 10 mins | Cook 2 mins

INGREDIENTS

20 ounces white chips*

10 ounces Reese's Peanut Butter Chips

20 ounces (about 2 1/2 cups) Jif creamy peanut butter

1 pinch of salt

*Do not use pure white chocolate to make this fudge. Use chips that contain palm kernel oil or use candy melts. We recommend Nestle® Premier White Morsels.

DIRECTIONS

1. Line an 8-inch square pan with non-stick tin foil or parchment paper.
2. Combine the white chips with the peanut butter chips in a large microwave-safe mixing bowl.
3. Heat on high power for 30-second increments, stirring after each, until melted.
4. Add the peanut butter and salt and stir until smooth.
5. Pour into the lined pan.
6. Let the fudge firm up at room temperature for about 8 hours before cutting into 24 squares.
7. Or freeze the fudge for 45 minutes, then remove and let thaw for one hour before cutting into squares.

NOTES

Make a large batch of this fudge by doubling the recipe and pouring it into a 9x13-inch pan.

chocolate peanut butter fudge

Serves 24 | Prep 10 mins | Cook 2 mins

INGREDIENTS

DIRECTIONS

Peanut Butter Fudge Layer

12 ounces white chips or white candy melts*

6 ounces peanut butter chips

12 ounces creamy peanut butter

1 pinch of salt

Chocolate Fudge Layer

2/3 cup heavy whipping cream

12 oz. dark chocolate chips

*We recommend using Nestle® Premier White Morsels.

1. Combine the white and peanut butter chips and heat for 30-second bursts of high power in the microwave, stirring after each, until melted.
2. Add peanut butter and salt and stir until well combined.
3. Pour into a parchment paper or non-stick tin foil-lined 8-inch square baking pan and set aside.
4. Heat the whipping cream on the stovetop set over medium heat just until it comes to a simmer.
5. Pour over the chocolate and let rest for 3 minutes before stirring until smooth.
6. Pour over the peanut butter fudge layer.
7. Draw a knife through the fudge to create swirls.
8. Cover and set aside at room temperature for 8 hours until the fudge firms up.
9. Remove the fudge and cut it into 24 pieces.

NOTES

Do not allow your cream to come to a boil or your chocolate fudge layer may become grainy.

vanilla fudge

Serves 25 | Prep 10 mins | Cook 1 1/2 mins

INGREDIENTS

16 ounces (2 ⅔ cups) white chocolate chips*

14 ounces (1 can) sweetened condensed milk

1 tablespoon vanilla extract

pinch salt

*If you use pure white chocolate which contains cocoa butter add an additional 2 ounces (⅓ cup).

DIRECTIONS

1. Line an 8 or 9-inch square baking pan with non-stick foil or lightly-greased parchment paper.
2. Combine the chocolate chips and sweetened condensed milk in a microwave-safe bowl.
3. Heat at 70% power for 90 seconds. Allow the bowl to rest in the warm microwave for 3 minutes.
4. Stir the chocolate until melted and smooth. If needed, heat 15 second increments at 70% power, stirring after each.
5. Stir in the vanilla extract and salt.
6. Pour the fudge evenly in the pan. Allow the fudge to cool at room temperature for about 8 hours or chill in the refrigerator until firm, about 3 hours.
7. Cut into 25 squares.

NOTES

This fudge is great with mix-ins! Try stirring in chopped nuts or dried fruits.

milk chocolate fudge

Serves 16 | Prep 10 mins | Cook 1 1/2 mins

INGREDIENTS

DIRECTIONS

16 ounces milk chocolate, finely chopped or chips

14 ounces sweetened condensed milk

1. Pour the milk chocolate chips and sweetened condensed milk into a microwave-safe mixing bowl.
2. Heat at 70% power for 90 seconds.
3. Let the bowl rest in the microwave for 3 minutes.
4. Remove and stir until melted.
5. If needed heat for another 15 seconds at 70% power. Let rest and stir.
6. Pour the fudge into a greased or lined 8-inch square baking pan.
7. Cover and chill in the refrigerator for 3 hours.
8. Remove the fudge from the pan and peel off the tin foil or parchment paper.
9. Cut into 16 pieces.

NOTES
Cut into smaller squares if desired. The large pieces make nice desserts.

mint chocolate chip fudge

Serves 25 | Prep 10 mins | Cook 1 1/2 mins

INGREDIENTS

16 ounces (2 ⅔ cups) white chocolate chips

14 ounces (1 can) sweetened condensed milk

1 1/2 teaspoons mint extract

pinch salt

green food coloring (optional)

⅔ cups mini semi-sweet chocolate chips, chilled

DIRECTIONS

1. Line an 8 or 9-inch square baking pan with non-stick foil or lightly-greased parchment paper.
2. Combine the chocolate and sweetened condensed milk in a microwave-safe bowl.
3. Heat at 70% power for 90 seconds. Allow the bowl to rest in the warm microwave for 3 minutes.
4. Stir the chocolate until melted. If needed, heat 15 second increments at 70% power, stirring after each.
5. Stir in the mint extract and salt.
6. Add a few drops of green food coloring, if desired.
7. Fold in the chilled mini chocolate chips
8. Pour the fudge evenly in the pan. Allow the fudge to cool at room temperature for about 8 hours or chill in the refrigerator until firm, about 3 hours.
9. Cut into 25 squares.

NOTES

Chilling the mini chocolate chips before stirring into the warm fudge keep the chips from melting.

frosting fudge

Serves 25 | Prep 10 mins | Cook 1 1/2 mins

INGREDIENTS

16 ounces white chocolate chips (2 ⅔ cups)

16 ounces (1 can) store-bought vanilla frosting

Optional ingredients:

1 pinch salt

DIRECTIONS

1. Line an 8 or 9-inch square baking pan with non-stick foil or lightly-greased parchment paper.
2. Combine the chocolate and frosting in a microwave safe bowl.
3. Heat at 70% power for 90 seconds.
4. Allow the bowl to rest in the warm microwave for 3 minutes.
5. Remove the bowl and stir the chocolate until melted.
6. If needed, heat 15 second increments at 70% power, stirring after each, until melted.
7. If using, stir in the salt.
8. Pour the fudge in an even layer in the pan.
9. Allow the fudge to cool at room temperature for about 8 hours or chill in the refrigerator until firm, about 3 hours.
10. Cut into 25 squares.

NOTES

Check out Fudge Basics for instructions to prepare this fudge on the stove-top!

marshmallow fudge

Serves 25 | Prep 10 mins | Cook 1 1/2 mins

INGREDIENTS

16 ounces (2 ⅔ cups) semi-sweet chocolate chips

14 ounces (1 can) sweetened condensed milk

1 jar (7 ounces) marshmallow creme (fluff)

1 teaspoon vanilla extract

pinch salt

1 ½ cups mini marshmallows

DIRECTIONS

1. Line an 8 or 9-inch square baking pan with non-stick foil or lightly-greased parchment paper.
2. Combine the chocolate, sweetened condensed milk, and marshmallow creme in a microwave-safe bowl.
3. Heat at 70% power for 90 seconds. Allow the bowl to rest in the warm microwave for 3 minutes.
4. Stir the chocolate until melted and smooth. If needed, heat 15 second increments at 70% power, stirring after each.
5. Stir in the vanilla extract and salt.
6. Gently fold in the marshmallows.
7. Pour the fudge evenly in the pan. Allow the fudge to cool at room temperature for about 8 hours or chill in the refrigerator until firm, about 3 hours.
8. Cut into 25 squares..

NOTES

If you like this fudge recipe, check out our rocky road fudge!

cookies and cream fudge

Serves 24 | Prep 10 mins | Cook 2 mins

INGREDIENTS

16 - 18 ounces white chocolate chips *

1 can (14-ounce) sweetened condensed milk

20 chocolate and vanilla creme sandwich cookies, broken into pieces

*If using pure white chips that contain cocoa butter use 18 ounces otherwise use 16 ounces.

DIRECTIONS

1. Pour the white chocolate chips and sweetened condensed milk into a microwave-safe mixing bowl.
2. Heat at 70% power for 90 seconds.
3. Let the bowl rest in the warm microwave for about 3 minutes then remove and stir.
4. If white chips are not all melted, repeat the process above, only heating for 15 seconds at 70% power.
5. Alternately, use the stovetop method listed on page 2.
6. Reserve about a third of the cookie pieces to sprinkle over the top of the fudge, then stir the rest into the fudge.
7. Pour the fudge into a greased or lined 8-inch square pan then sprinkle the reserved cookie pieces over top.
8. Cover and chill for 3-4 hours or until firm.
9. Remove the fudge and cut into 36 squares.

NOTES

Swap out lemon, mint, red velvet, or any other flavored sandwich cookie for the chocolate cookies.

butterscotch fudge

Serves 24 | Prep 10 mins | Cook 2 mins

INGREDIENTS

DIRECTIONS

3 cups butterscotch chips*

14 ounces (1 can) sweetened condensed milk

1 pinch salt

* Add an additional 1/4 cup butterscotch chips if using a thin store brand of sweetened condensed milk.

1. Line an 8-inch square pan with non-stick tin foil or parchment paper.
2. Stir together the butterscotch chips, sweetened condensed milk, and salt in a large microwave-safe mixing bowl.
3. Heat at 70% power for 90 seconds.
4. Let the bowl rest in the microwave for 5 minutes.
5. Remove and stir slowly until melted and smooth.
6. Alternately, use the stovetop method listed on page 2.
7. Pour into the prepared pan and spread into an even layer.
8. Cover with plastic wrap or tin foil and refrigerate for about 3 hours until firm.
9. Remove from pan, peel off the tin foil or parchment paper, and cut fudge into 36 small squares.

NOTES

You can also just let the fudge firm up at room temperature. This might take up to 5 or 6 hours.

chocolate coconut fudge

Serves 24 | Prep 10 mins | Cook 2 mins

INGREDIENTS

22 oz semi-sweet or bittersweet chocolate

15 oz can of cream of coconut

3 tbsp shredded sweetened coconut

DIRECTIONS

1. Line an 8 or 9-inch square pan with tin foil or parchment paper.
2. Melt the chocolate chips using a double boiler or in the microwave.
3. Allow the chocolate to cool, stirring often, until just warm to the touch.
4. Stir the cream of coconut until it is well combined then pour it over the warm chocolate.
5. Stir until blended then pour into the prepared pan.
6. Sprinkle the shredded coconut over top of the fudge.
7. Cover pan and chill in the refrigerator for 3-4 hours until firm.
8. Remove and cut into 24 pieces.

NOTES
For more depth of flavor toast the coconut in a skillet set over low heat, stirring until golden brown.

maple fudge

Serves 36 | Prep 10 mins | Cook 3 mins

INGREDIENTS

DIRECTIONS

24-28 oz white chocolate chips*

3/4 cup pancake syrup

optional, pinch of salt

*If using pure white chocolate which has cocoa butter listed in the ingredients use 28 ounces. If using white chips that do not contain cocoa butter, like Nestle® Premier White Morsels, use 24 ounces.

1. Melt the white chocolate in the microwave using 30 second bursts of high power, stirring after each, until melted. (Alternatively, you can melt the white chocolate in a double boiler set over low heat on the stove.)
2. Pour the maple syrup and pinch of salt, if using, into the white chocolate and stir slowly until well combined and thickened.
3. Spread into an 8-inch square pan that has been lined with non-stick tin foil, parchment paper, or tin foil that has been sprayed with baking spray.
4. Cover and chill for 3-4 hours until firm.
5. Then remove from the pan and cut into 36 pieces.

NOTES

If you prefer you can use 3/4 cup plus 2 tablespoons of pure maple syrup.
.

nutty & fruity fudge

rocky road fudge

Serves 25 | Prep 15 mins | Cook 1 1/2 mins

INGREDIENTS

12 ounces (2 cups) semi-sweet chocolate chips

14 ounces (1 can) sweetened condensed milk

1 teaspoon vanilla extract

pinch salt

1 ½ cups coarsely chopped walnuts or peanuts

3 cups mini marshmallows

DIRECTIONS

1. Line an 8 or 9-inch square baking pan with non-stick foil or lightly-greased parchment paper.
2. Combine the chocolate chips and sweetened condensed milk in a microwave-safe bowl.
3. Heat at 70% power for 90 seconds. Allow the bowl to rest in the warm microwave for 3 minutes.
4. Stir the chocolate until melted and smooth. If needed, heat 15 second increments at 70% power, stirring after each.
5. Mix in the extract, salt, and nuts. Fold in the marshmallows.
6. Pour the fudge evenly in the pan.
7. Allow the fudge to cool at room temperature for about 8 hours or chill in the refrigerator until firm, about 3 hours.
8. Cut into 25 squares.

NOTES

Check out Fudge Basics for instructions to prepare this fudge on the stove-top!

butter pecan fudge

Serves 25 | Prep 10 mins | Cook 1 1/2 mins

INGREDIENTS

3 tablespoons butter, browned

1 ½ tablespoons butter

1 ½ cups pecans, chopped

18 ounces (3 cups) white chocolate chips

14 ounces (1 can) sweetened condensed milk

1 teaspoon vanilla extract

pinch salt

1 teaspoon cinnamon

DIRECTIONS

1. Line an 8 or 9-inch square baking pan with non-stick foil or lightly-greased parchment paper.
2. Melt 1 ½ tablespoons butter in a saucepan, add the pecans, mix well and heat until toasted, 3-4 minutes. Overturn on a baking tray and cool.
3. Combine the chocolate and milk in a microwave safe bowl. Heat at 70% power for 90 seconds and rest in the warm microwave for 3 minutes. Stir until smooth.
4. Stir in the vanilla, salt, and cinnamon, then the browned butter. Fold in the pecans.
5. Pour the fudge in an even layer in the pan.
6. Allow the fudge to cool at room temperature for about 8 hours or chill in the refrigerator until firm, about 3 hours.
7. Cut into 25 squares.

NOTES

To brown butter, place the butter in a light-colored saucepan over medium heat. Swirl pan occasionally. Heat until butter darkens to a deep brown, several minutes.

chocolate cashew butter fudge

Serves 16 | Prep 10 mins | Cook 5 mins

INGREDIENTS

16 ounces semi-sweet chocolate, finely chopped or chips

12 ounces cashew butter, well stirred

1/2 cup chopped cashews

DIRECTIONS

1. Pour chopped chocolate into a microwave-safe bowl or in the bowl of a double boiler.
2. Heat on high power for 30-second increments, stirring after each until 75% of the chocolate is melted or melt in a double boiler on the stovetop set over low heat.
3. Remove the chocolate from the heat and continue to stir the chocolate until all of the chunks have melted.
4. Stir in the cashew butter.
5. Pour into a non-stick tin foil-lined or parchment paper-lined 8-inch square pan.
6. Sprinkle chopped cashews over top.
7. Cover and chill in the refrigerator for 3 hours until firm.
8. Remove and allow to warm to room temperature before cutting into 25 squares.

NOTES
You can swap out almond butter or peanut butter to make a variety of nut butter fudge flavors.

maple walnut fudge

Serves 25 | Prep 15 mins | Cook 1 1/2 mins

INGREDIENTS	DIRECTIONS
16 ounces (2 ⅔ cups) white chocolate chips 14 ounces (1 can) sweetened condensed milk 1 ½ teaspoons maple extract pinch salt 1 ½ cups coarsely chopped walnuts	1. Line an 8 or 9-inch square baking pan with non-stick foil or lightly-greased parchment paper. 2. Combine the chocolate and sweetened condensed milk in a microwave-safe bowl. 3. Heat at 70% power for 90 seconds. Allow the bowl to rest in the warm microwave for 3 minutes. 4. Stir the chocolate until melted. If needed, heat 15 second increments at 70% power, stirring after each. 5. Mix in the salt and extract and fold in the walnuts. 6. Pour the fudge evenly in the pan. 7. Allow the fudge to cool at room temperature for about 8 hours or chill in the refrigerator until firm, about 3 hours. 8. Cut into 25 squares.

NOTES

Check out Fudge Basics for instructions to prepare this fudge on the stove-top!

pumpkin fudge

Serves 25 | Prep 15 mins | Cook 1 1/2 mins

INGREDIENTS

24 ounces (4 cups) white chocolate chips

½ cup pumpkin puree (NOT pumpkin pie filling)

2 teaspoons pumpkin pie spice

½ teaspoon vanilla extract

pinch salt

1 cup coarsely chopped pecans (optional)

DIRECTIONS

1. Line an 8 or 9-inch square baking pan with non-stick foil or lightly-greased parchment paper.
2. Combine the chocolate and pumpkin puree in a microwave-safe bowl.
3. Heat at 70% power for 90 seconds. Allow the bowl to rest in the warm microwave for 3 minutes.
4. Stir the chocolate until melted and smooth. If needed, heat 15 second increments at 70% power, stirring after each.
5. Mix in the spice, extract, and salt.
6. Pour the fudge evenly in the pan, and gently press pecans into the top of the fudge.
7. Allow the fudge to cool at room temperature for about 8 hours or chill in the refrigerator until firm, about 3 hours.
8. Cut into 25 squares.

NOTES

This is a great fudge to serve throughout the fall season.

lemon fudge

Serves 36 | Prep 10 mins | Cook 2 mins

INGREDIENTS

24-28 oz white chocolate chips*

1 1/3 cup lemon curd

*If using pure white chocolate which has cocoa butter listed in the ingredients use 28 ounces. If using white chips that do not contain cocoa butter, like Nestle® Premier White Morsels, use 24 ounces.

DIRECTIONS

1. Pour the white chocolate chips and the lemon curd into a microwave-safe mixing bowl.
2. Heat at 70% power for 1 minute 45 seconds.
3. Let the bowl rest in the microwave for 3 minutes.
4. Remove and stir until melted.
5. If needed, heat for another 15 seconds at 70% power. Let rest, allowing the residual heat in the fudge to melt any remaining chips, then stir until melted.
6. Pour the fudge into a greased or lined 8-inch baking pan.
7. Cover with a piece of tin foil or plastic wrap.
8. Chill in the refrigerator for 3-4 hours until firm.
9. Remove the fudge from the pan and cut into 36 squares.

NOTES

You can add a tablespoon of fresh lemon zest to enhance the lemon flavor.

strawberry fudge

Serves 36 | Prep 10 mins | Cook 3 mins

INGREDIENTS

24-28 oz white chocolate chips*

11.75 ounces strawberry ice cream topping

1 teaspoon lemon juice

1 pinch salt

*If using pure white chocolate use 28 ounces. If using white chips like Nestle® Premier White Morsels or candy melts use 24 ounces.

DIRECTIONS

1. Melt the white chocolate chips in the microwave using 30 second bursts of high power, stirring after each until melted or melt using a double boiler set over low heat.
2. Pour the strawberry topping, lemon juice, and pinch of salt into the melted white chocolate.
3. Stir until well combined.
4. Pour into a well-greased or a non-stick tin foil-lined 8-inch square baking pan.
5. Cover and chill for 3-4 hours until firm.
6. Remove from the pan and cut into 36 squares.
7. Wrap in wax paper and place in a zip-top bag or in an airtight container and store in the refrigerator for up to 2 weeks or in the freezer for up to 3 months.

NOTES

You can also use preserves or jam in place of the ice cream topping to make fruity fudge.

creamsicle fudge

Serves 25 | Prep 15 mins | Cook 1 1/2 mins

INGREDIENTS

16 ounces (2 ⅔ cups) white chocolate chips*

16 ounces (1 can) store-bought vanilla frosting

1 ½ teaspoons orange extract

orange food coloring

*If you use pure white chocolate which contains cocoa butter add an additional 2 ounces (⅓ cup).

NOTES

Check out Fudge Basics for instructions to prepare this fudge on the stove-top!

DIRECTIONS

1. Line an 8 or 9-inch square baking pan with non-stick foil or lightly-greased parchment paper.
2. Combine the chocolate and frosting in a microwave-safe bowl.
3. Heat at 70% power for 90 seconds. Allow the bowl to rest in the warm microwave for 3 minutes.
4. Stir the chocolate until melted and smooth.
5. Stir in orange extract.
6. Pour ⅓ of the mixture into a separate bowl. Color the remaining mixture with drops of orange food coloring.
7. Pour the orange mixture evenly in the pan. Pour the remaining white fudge on top. Use a knife or toothpick to swirl the colors together.
8. Allow the fudge to cool at room temperature for about 8 hours or chill in the refrigerator until firm, about 3 hours.
9. Cut into 25 squares.

key lime fudge

Serves 36 | Prep 10 mins | Cook 2 mins

INGREDIENTS

DIRECTIONS

24-28 oz white chocolate chips*

1 1/3 cup key lime curd

*If using pure white chocolate which has cocoa butter listed in the ingredients use 28 ounces. If using white chips that do not contain cocoa butter, like Nestle® Premier White Morsels, use 24 ounces.

1. Pour the white chocolate chips and the key lime curd into a microwave-safe mixing bowl.
2. Heat at 70% power for 1 minute 45 seconds.
3. Let the bowl rest in the microwave for 3 minutes.
4. Remove and stir until melted.
5. If needed, heat for another 15 seconds at 70% power. Let rest, allowing the residual heat in the fudge to melt any remaining chips, then stir until melted.
6. Pour the fudge into a greased or lined 8-inch baking pan.
7. Cover with a piece of tin foil or plastic wrap.
8. Chill in the refrigerator for 3-4 hours until firm.
9. Remove the fudge from the pan and cut into 36 squares.

NOTES

If you are unable to find key lime curd, traditional lime curd tastes great in this fudge too.

dark chocolate raspberry fudge

Serves 25 | Prep 15 mins | Cook 3 mins

INGREDIENTS

12 ounces (2 cups) dark chocolate chips

12 ounces (2 cups) white chocolate chips

8 ounces (½ can) dark chocolate frosting

8 ounces (½ can) white or vanilla frosting

⅓ cup raspberry preserves or jam

DIRECTIONS

1. Line an 8 or 9-inch square baking pan with non-stick foil or lightly-greased parchment paper.
2. Combine the dark chocolate chips and chocolate frosting in a microwave-safe bowl.
3. Heat at 70% power for 90 seconds. Allow the bowl to rest in the warm microwave for 3 minutes. Stir the chocolate until smooth.
4. Pour the fudge in an even layer in the pan. If thin, refrigerate for one hour before adding the next layer.
5. Melt the white chocolate chips and vanilla frosting, and stir until smooth.
6. Stir in the raspberry preserves. Pour in an even layer on top of the chocolate layer.
7. Allow the fudge to cool at room temperature for about 8 hours or chill in the refrigerator until firm, about 3 hours.
8. Cut into 25 squares.

NOTES
Visit Fudge Basics to learn how to make this fudge on the stove-top.

New Year's Eve countdown clock fudge

Serves 32 | Prep 10 mins | Cook 2 mins

INGREDIENTS

24-28 ounces white chocolate chips*

14 ounces sweetened condensed milk

1 teaspoon almond extract

1 pinch salt

*Use 24 ounces chips made with palm kernel oil OR 28 ounces of pure white chocolate made with cocoa butter

DIRECTIONS

1. Combine the white chocolate and sweetened condensed milk in a large microwave-safe bowl.
2. Heat at 70% power for 1 minute 45 seconds, then let the bowl rest in the microwave for 3 minutes.
3. Add the almond extract and salt then stir until melted.
4. If needed, heat for additional 15 seconds at 70% power, allowing the fudge to rest before stirring until completely melted.
5. Cover the bowl and set aside for 4 hours until firm.
6. Scoop out 1-ounce (2 tablespoons) of white chocolate fudge and roll into a ball then flatten into a 2 1/4 inch diameter disk. Repeat creating 32 disks.
7. Using a black food coloring marker, draw a clock design onto each round piece of fudge.
8. Allow the food coloring to dry completely.

NOTES

Draw the hands on the clock so that it looks like its just before midnight.

fudge hearts

Serves 12 | Prep 60 mins | Cook 1 1/2 mins

INGREDIENTS

12 ounces (1 bag) pink candy melts

½ cup of a can of sweetened condensed milk

Supplies:

disposable piping bag

size 1M decorating tip

DIRECTIONS

1. Prepare a piping bag with 1M tip and set aside. Line a baking tray with wax or parchment paper.
2. Combine the candy melts and sweetened condensed milk in a microwave-safe bowl.
3. Heat at 70% power for 90 seconds. Allow the bowl to rest in the warm microwave for 3 minutes.
4. Stir the mixture until smooth. If needed, heat 15 second increments at 70% power, stirring after each.
5. Let the mixture sit at room temperature until it thickens to the consistency of frosting, stirring every 5 minutes. This may take 30 to 45 minutes.
6. Fill the decorating bag and close with a rubber band. Pipe hearts on the baking tray.
7. Chill in the refrigerator 3 hours.

NOTES

Be patient! Make sure your fudge thickens enough to hold its shape when piped. Find piping bags, decorating tips, and candy melts at the craft store or online.

strawberry frosting fudge

Serves 25　|　Prep 15 mins　|　Cook 1 1/2 mins

INGREDIENTS

DIRECTIONS

16 ounces (2 ⅔ cups) white chocolate chips

12 ounces (1 can) store-bought strawberry frosting

heart sprinkles (optional)

1. Line an 8 or 9-inch baking pan with non-stick foil or lightly greased parchment paper.
2. Place the chocolate chips and strawberry frosting in a microwave-safe bowl.
3. Heat at 70% power for 90 seconds. Allow the bowl to rest in the warm microwave for 3 minutes. Stir until the chocolate is melted and smooth.
4. Pour evenly in the prepared baking pan.
5. Top with heart sprinkles.
6. Allow the fudge to cool at room temperature for about 8 hours or chill in the refrigerator until firm, about 3 hours.
7. Cut into squares.

NOTES

Adding heart sprinkles on top makes this a fun and easy Valentine's day treat.

rainbow fudge

Serves 25 | Prep 1 hour 15 mins | Cook 9 mins

INGREDIENTS

36 ounces (6 cups) white chocolate chips

28 ounces (2 cans) sweetened condensed milk

gel paste food coloring (red, orange, yellow, green, blue, and purple)

DIRECTIONS

1. Line an 8-inch baking pan with non-stick foil or lightly greased parchment paper.
2. Divide the condensed milk into 6 microwave-safe bowls. (Each bowl will have about ⅓ cup plus 1 tablespoon.)
3. Pour 1 cup of white chocolate chips in each bowl.
4. Heat one bowl at 70% power for 90 seconds. Allow the bowl to rest in the warm microwave for 3 minutes. Stir until the chocolate is melted and smooth.
5. Stir in purple food coloring and spread the mixture evenly in the baking pan. Freeze for 10 minutes.
6. While the tray is in the freezer, prepare blue fudge. Layer on top of the purple.
7. Repeat with every color.
8. Chill in the refrigerator 3 hours then cut into squares.

NOTES

Find gel paste food colorings in the craft store or online. The brand used here is Americolor Soft Gel Pastes. I use an 8-inch baking pan to be sure each color isn't spread too thinly.

Easter orange fudge carrots

Serves 12 | Prep 10 mins | Cook 1 1/2 mins

INGREDIENTS

Orange fudge

20 ounces orange candy melts

14 ounce can of sweetened condensed milk

1 1/2 teaspoons orange extract

Optional: orange food coloring

Candy Carrot Greens

6 ounces green candy melts, melted

DIRECTIONS

1. Combine the orange candy melts and sweetened condensed milk in a large microwave-safe bowl.
2. Heat at 70% power for 90 seconds then let the bowl rest in the microwave for 3 minutes.
3. Add the orange extract and coloring then stir until melted.
4. If needed heat for 15 more seconds then stir.
5. Pour the fudge into a tin foil-lined 8-inch round pan.
6. Cover and refrigerate for 3-4 hours until firm.
7. Remove fudge from pan and cut into 12 wedges.
8. Pipe 24 stems and squiggles of green Candy Melts onto parchment paper creating carrot greens.
9. Freeze for 2-3 minutes until the candy hardens.
10. Poke two holes into the flat ends of each fudge carrot using a wooden skewer or toothpick.
11. Insert a green candy stem into each hole.

NOTES

It's best to make more greens than needed as they may break when inserting into the fudge.

red, white, and blue fudge

Serves 25 | Prep 15 mins | Cook 1 1/2 mins

INGREDIENTS

16 ounces (2 ⅔ cups) white chocolate chips

14 ounces (1 can) sweetened condensed milk

pinch of salt

gel paste food coloring (red, white, and blue)

DIRECTIONS

1. Line an 8-inch baking pan with non-stick foil or lightly greased parchment paper.
2. Place the chocolate and sweetened condensed milk in a microwave-safe bowl.
3. Heat at 70% power for 90 seconds. Allow the bowl to rest in the warm microwave for 3 minutes. Stir until the chocolate is melted and smooth.
4. Stir in the salt.
5. Divide the mixture into three bowls: Use the most for white, and smaller amounts for blue and red.
6. Add food coloring to each bowl and stir.
7. Scrape the blue mixture in the pan, then the white, then the red. Use a toothpick to swirl the fudge.
8. Chill in the refrigerator 3 hours then cut into squares.

NOTES

Find gel paste food colorings in the craft store or online. The brand used here is Americolor Soft Gel Pastes. You don't *need* white food coloring, but it brightens the fudge nicely.

zombie fudge

Serves 25 | Prep 20 mins | Cook 1 1/2 mins

INGREDIENTS

24 ounces green candy melts (2 bags)

14 ounces (1 can) sweetened condensed milk

zombie hands sprinkles

candy eyes

red food coloring pen

chocolate sprinkles

tube red gel icing (optional)

DIRECTIONS

1. Line an 8-inch baking pan with non-stick foil or lightly greased parchment paper.
2. Place the candy melts and sweetened condensed milk in a microwave-safe bowl.
3. Heat at 70% power for 90 seconds. Allow the bowl to rest in the warm microwave for 3 minutes. Stir until the chocolate is melted and smooth.
4. Pour evenly in the prepared baking pan.
5. Pour some chocolate sprinkles in scattered piles and insert zombie hands. Use the pen to make the candy eyes bloodshot and scatter on fudge. Add icing "blood."
6. Allow the fudge to cool at room temperature for about 8 hours or chill in the refrigerator until firm, about 3 hours.
7. Cut into squares.

NOTES

Find the candy melts, sprinkles, and food coloring pen at the craft store or online. Most supermarkets carry red gel icing.

milk chocolate fudge turkeys

Serves 16 | Prep 10 mins | Cook 1 1/2 mins

INGREDIENTS

16 ounces milk chocolate, finely chopped or chips

14 ounces sweetened condensed milk

32 large candy eyes

2 ounces red candy melts, melted

2 ounces orange candy melts, melted

Food-use-only paintbrush

DIRECTIONS

1. Pour the milk chocolate and sweetened condensed milk into a microwave-safe mixing bowl.
2. Heat at 70% power for 90 seconds.
3. Let the bowl rest in the microwave for 3 minutes.
4. Remove and stir until melted.
5. Pour the fudge into a lined 8-inch pan.
6. Cover and chill in the refrigerator for 3 hours or at room temperature for 6-8 hours.
7. Remove the fudge from the pan and cut into 16 squares.
8. Use a paintbrush to paint an orange beak and a red wattle in the center of each square of fudge.
9. Freeze for 2 minutes until the candy melts harden.
10. Attach two large candy eyes to the fudge above the beak and wattle using candy melts then repeat.

NOTES

The candy eyes will soften as they wick up moisture from the fudge making these easy to bite into.

peanut blossom fudge

Serves 36 | Prep 20 mins | Cook 1 1/2 mins

INGREDIENTS

2 1/2 cups peanut butter chips

14 ounces sweetened condensed milk

1 pinch of salt

1/2 cup creamy peanut butter

1/2 cup brown sugar, sifted

36 Hershey's Kisses

DIRECTIONS

1. Stir together peanut butter chips, sweetened condensed milk, salt, and creamy peanut butter.
2. Heat in the microwave at 70% power for 90 seconds.
3. Let the bowl rest in the microwave for 3 minutes.
4. Stir until melted.
5. If needed, heat at 70% power for 10-15 second increments to melt all the peanut butter chips.
6. Use an ice cream scoop or a spoon to scoop out 36 tablespoons of the fudge.
7. Roll one of the fudge scoops into a ball and roll it in the brown sugar then set it on a parchment paper lined pan.
8. Immediately insert a Hershey's Kiss allowing the fudge to flatten into a disc and to crack slightly.
9. Repeat.

NOTES

Push the brown sugar through a fine mesh sieve in order to break up any clumps.

peppermint bark fudge

Serves 16 | Prep 10 mins | Cook 3 mins

INGREDIENTS

6 ounces semi-sweet chocolate, finely chopped or chips (about 1 cup)

14 ounces (1 can) sweetened condensed milk, DIVIDED

10 ounces white chocolate

1 teaspoon peppermint extract

2-3 tablespoons peppermint candy cane pieces

DIRECTIONS

1. Combine the semi-sweet chocolate with 2/3 cup of the sweetened condensed milk.
2. Heat in the microwave at 70% power for 75 seconds, then let the bowl rest in the microwave for 3 minutes.
3. If needed heat an additional 10-15 seconds.
4. Remove and stir slowly until all the chocolate melts.
5. Spread into a foil or paper lined 8-inch square pan.
6. Combine the white chocolate with the remaining sweetened condensed milk.
7. Heat at 70% power for 80 seconds, let rest, 3 minutes.
8. Pour in the peppermint extract and stir until smooth.
9. Spread over the chocolate fudge layer then immediately sprinkle on the crushed candy canes.
10. Cover and set aside for about 6 hours until the peppermint bark fudge is firm then cut into 16 squares.

NOTES

This fudge will stay fresh for 2 weeks, however the candy canes will become sticky in a few days.

eggnog fudge

Serves 36 | Prep 10 mins | Cook 3 mins

INGREDIENTS

24 ounces pure white chocolate (that contains cocoa butter), finely chopped

1/4 cup sweetened condensed milk

7 tablespoons egg nog

1/4 teaspoon freshly grated nutmeg

1/2 teaspoon eggnog flavoring or rum extract

DIRECTIONS

1. Stir together the white chocolate, sweetened condensed milk, eggnog, and half of the nutmeg.
2. Heat in the microwave on 70% power for 90 seconds.
3. Remove and stir.
4. Heat on 70% power for 30 seconds then let the bowl sit in the microwave for about 3 minutes before stirring.
5. If needed, heat for 15-second increments until melted.
6. Stir in the eggnog flavoring or rum extract.
7. Spread into a greased or lined 8-inch square pan.
8. Sprinkle the remaining nutmeg over top.
9. Cover and refrigerate for 3-4 hours.
10. Remove from pan and cut into 36 squares.

NOTES

You can pour the fudge into an 8-inch by 4-inch loaf pan and cut it into slices for a different look.

chocolate peppermint fudge

Serves 36 | Prep 10 mins | Cook 1 1/2 mins

INGREDIENTS

12 oz semi-sweet chocolate finely chopped or chips

14 oz (1 can) Sweetened Condensed Milk

1 teaspoon peppermint extract

1/3 cup Andes Peppermint Crunch Baking Bits

DIRECTIONS

1. Combine the chocolate and sweetened condensed milk.
2. Heat in the microwave at 70% power for 90 seconds.
3. Then let the bowl rest in the microwave for 3 minutes before stirring until smooth.
4. Add the peppermint extract and stir just to incorporate.
5. Pour into greased or lined 8-inch square pan.
6. Sprinkle the Andes Peppermint Crunch Baking Bits over top and gently press them into the fudge.
7. Cover and chill in the refrigerator for at 2-3 hours or set aside for 6-8 hours until the fudge firms up.
8. Remove from pan and cut into 36 pieces.

NOTES

If you prefer to use peppermint oil cut the amount to ½ teaspoon.

fudge snowmen

Serves 16 | **Prep 10 mins** | Cook 2 mins

INGREDIENTS

20 ounces white candy melts or white chips made with palm kernel oil
OR
24 ounces *pure* white chocolate

14 ounces sweetened condensed milk

1 teaspoon almond extract

1 pinch salt

112 mini chocolate chips

16 carrot sprinkles

DIRECTIONS

1. Combine the white chocolate and sweetened condensed milk in a large microwave-safe bowl.
2. Heat at 70% power for 90 seconds, then let rest in the microwave for 3 minutes then stir until melted.
3. Heat for 15 seconds more if needed.
4. Stir in the almond extract and salt.
5. Spread evenly into the prepared pan.
6. Cover and refrigerate for 3-4 hours until firm.
7. Remove the fudge from the pan.
8. Trim the edges of the fudge then cut into 16 squares.
9. Press 2 mini chocolate chips and one orange carrot sprinkle into a square of fudge to create the snowman's eyes and nose.
10. Form a curved smile using 5 mini chocolate chips below the carrot nose.

NOTES

If you can't find orange carrot sprinkles you can use orange candy coated sunflower seeds.

fudge reindeer

Serves 16 | Prep 10 mins | Cook 1 1/2 mins

INGREDIENTS

2 1/2 cups peanut butter chips

14 ounces (1 can) sweetened condensed milk

1 pinch of salt

1/2 cup creamy peanut butter

4 ounces melted dark cocoa candy melts

16 Red M&M's
32 candy eyes
1 teaspoon clear piping gel

DIRECTIONS

1. Stir together peanut butter chips, sweetened condensed milk, salt, and creamy peanut butter.
2. Heat in the microwave at 70% power for 90 seconds.
3. Let the bowl rest in the microwave for 3 minutes, then stir until melted.
4. Spread into a greased or lined pan then chill until firm for about 3-4 hours.
5. Trim the edges of the fudge then cut into 16 squares.
6. Using melted dark cocoa candy melts, pipe 32 (1 inch long) antlers on a parchment paper-lined baking sheet.
7. Freeze for about 3 minutes just until firm.
8. Remove and use clear piping gel to attach one red M&M nose and two candy eyes to each fudge square.
9. Attach two antlers to each reindeer fudge using piping gel or insert the antlers on either side of the fudge.

NOTES

If you don't have piping gel you can attach the decorations using melted peanut butter chips.

easy Christmas fudge

Serves 25 | Prep 10 mins | Cook 2 mins

INGREDIENTS

20-24 ounces white chocolate chips*

14 ounces sweetened condensed milk

1 teaspoon almond extract

1 pinch salt

1/2 cup Christmas sprinkles

*Use 20 ounces chips made with palm kernel oil OR 24 ounces pure white chocolate made with cocoa butter

DIRECTIONS

1. Combine the white chocolate and sweetened condensed milk in a large microwave-safe bowl.
2. Heat at 70% power for 90 seconds, then let the bowl rest in the microwave for 3 minutes.
3. Add the almond extract and salt then stir until melted.
4. If needed, heat for additional 10-15 seconds at 70% power, allowing the fudge to rest before stirring until completely melted.
5. Spread evenly into an 8-inch square pan.
6. Top with red, white, and green sprinkles.
7. Tap the pan on the counter a few times to ensure the sprinkles have attached to the fudge.
8. Cover and refrigerate for 3-4 hours or set aside at room temperature for 6-8 hours until firm.
9. Remove from pan and cut into 25 squares.

NOTES

You can use other extracts, like vanilla, peppermint, coconut, lemon, or orange to flavor fudge.

"Oh, fudge!" soap fudge

Serves 6 to 8 | Prep 30 mins | Cook 1 1/2 mins

INGREDIENTS

16 ounces (2 ⅔ cups) white chocolate chips

14 ounces (1 can) sweetened condensed milk.

pinch salt (optional)

red food coloring

DIRECTIONS

1. Combine the chocolate and sweetened condensed milk in a microwave-safe bowl.
2. Heat at 70% power for 90 seconds. Allow the bowl to rest in the warm microwave for 3 minutes.
3. Stir the chocolate until melted. If needed, heat 15 second increments at 70% power.
4. Stir in salt, if using.
5. Pour the fudge into food-safe silicone soap molds. You will have 6 or 8, depending on the size of your mold.
6. Chill in the refrigerator until firm, about 3 hours.
7. Remove from the mold. Use stone stamps to spell "Lifebuoy" or "Oh fudge" on the fudge.

NOTES

For this recipe, you'll also need a silicone soap mold and alphabet stone stamps. This fudge is a great gift for fans of the movie, "A Christmas Story!"

unconventional fudge

caramel fudge

Serves 25 | Prep 10 mins | Cook 1 1/2 mins

INGREDIENTS

24 - 28 ounces white chocolate chips*

12 ounces caramel sauce

optional: salt

*If using pure white chocolate (with cocoa butter listed in the ingredients) use 28 ounces. Otherwise, use 24 ounces.

DIRECTIONS

1. Pour the white chocolate chips and caramel sauce into a microwave-safe mixing bowl.
2. Heat at 70% power for 1 minute then stir.
3. Heat for another 45 seconds then let the bowl rest in the microwave for 3 minutes.
4. Remove and stir until melted.
5. If needed heat for another 15 seconds at 70% power.
6. Let rest and stir.
7. Pour the fudge into a lined or greased 8-inch baking pan.
8. Optional: sprinkle with salt.
9. Cover and chill in the refrigerator for 3-4 hours.
10. Remove the fudge from the pan and cut into 25 squares.

NOTES

This fudge is soft and a bit sticky, much like caramel. Use Dulce de Leche for a firmer fudge.

cake batter funfetti fudge

Serves 36 | Prep 10 mins | Cook 2 mins

INGREDIENTS

20-24 ounces white chocolate chips*

14 ounces sweetened condensed milk

1 teaspoon cake batter flavoring

1/3 cup rainbow sprinkles

*If using pure white chocolate (that contains cocoa butter) use 24 ounces. Otherwise, use 20 ounces.

DIRECTIONS

1. Stir together the white chocolate chips and the sweetened condensed milk.
2. Heat at 70% power for 90 seconds.
3. Let the bowl rest in the warm microwave for 3 minutes.
4. Remove and stir until melted.
5. If needed, heat for 10-second bursts of 70% power, stirring after each, until melted.
6. Stir in the cake batter flavoring & 1/4 cup of the sprinkles.
7. Spread the fudge into a greased or lined 8-inch pan.
8. Toss the remaining sprinkles over top and gently press them down into the fudge using your hand.
9. Cover the fudge and chill in the refrigerator for 3-4 hours until the fudge firms up.
10. Remove from the pan and cut into 36 squares.

NOTES

This fudge is great to make with holiday colored sprinkles too.

mermaid fudge

Serves 25 | Prep 15 mins | Cook 1 1/2 mins

INGREDIENTS

16 ounces (2 ⅔ cups) white chocolate chips

14 ounces (1 can) sweetened condensed milk

teal food coloring

blue food coloring (optional)

mermaid sprinkle mix

DIRECTIONS

1. Line an 8 or 9-inch square baking pan with non-stick foil or lightly-greased parchment paper.
2. Combine the chocolate chips and condensed milk in a microwave-safe bowl.
3. Heat at 70% power for 90 seconds. Allow the bowl to rest in the warm microwave for 3 minutes.
4. Stir the chocolate until melted and smooth.
5. Pour a bit of the mixture into a small bowl, add blue food coloring, and stir well.
6. Stir teal coloring into the rest of the fudge and mix well.
7. Pour the teal fudge evenly in the pan. Pour the blue fudge all over the top and swirl with a toothpick.
8. Generously sprinkle the mermaid mix on top.
9. Chill in the refrigerator until firm, about 3 hours.
10. Cut into 25 squares.

NOTES

For an even easier fudge, skip the blue and make the whole batch teal! For food coloring, I recommend Americolor Soft Gel Pastes in Teal and Sky Blue.

chocolate peanut butter cup fudge

Serves 25 | Prep 10 mins | Cook 1 1/2 mins

INGREDIENTS

16 ounces (2 ⅔ cups) semi-sweet chocolate chips

16 ounces (1 can) store-bought chocolate frosting

1 ½ cups coarsely chopped chocolate peanut butter cups

DIRECTIONS

1. Line an 8 or 9-inch square baking pan with non-stick foil or lightly-greased parchment paper.
2. Combine the chocolate chips and frosting in a microwave-safe bowl.
3. Heat at 70% power for 90 seconds. Allow the bowl to rest in the warm microwave for 3 minutes.
4. Stir the chocolate until melted and smooth. If needed, heat 15 second increments at 70% power, stirring after each.
5. Stir in the chocolate peanut butter cups. If desired, add extra candy pieces on top of the fudge.
6. Pour the fudge evenly in the pan. Allow the fudge to cool at room temperature for about 8 hours or chill in the refrigerator until firm, about 3 hours.
7. Cut into 25 squares.

NOTES

In place of the frosting, you may use a 14-ounce can of sweetened condensed milk.

cookie butter fudge

Serves 36 | Prep 10 mins | Cook 3 mins

INGREDIENTS

18 ounce white candy melts
OR
21 ounces pure white chocolate

14 ounces speculoos cookie butter

Optional: 6-10 speculoos cookies, broken into small pieces

DIRECTIONS

1. Melt white chocolate in the microwave using 30-second bursts of high power, stirring after each until melted, or on the stove using a double boiler set over low heat.
2. Add the Biscoff Cookie Butter to the white chocolate and stir until well combined.
3. Pour into a non-stick tin foil or parchment paper-lined 8-inch square baking pan and spread into an even layer.
4. If using, sprinkle the cookie pieces over the fudge.
5. Cover and let sit at room temperature for 4 hours or freeze for 45 minutes, then let sit at room temperature for about an hour before cutting into 36 pieces.

NOTES

Biscoff®, a popular brand of speculoos cookies and spread, is available in many grocery stores.

chocolate hazelnut spread fudge

Serves 36 | Prep 10 mins | Cook 1 1/2 mins

INGREDIENTS

18 ounces milk chocolate, finely chopped pieces or chips

1 ½ cups hazelnut spread with cocoa

Optional ingredients:

1 teaspoon pure vanilla extract or vanilla bean paste

1 pinch salt

DIRECTIONS

1. Melt the milk chocolate in the microwave using 30-second bursts of high power, stirring after each until melted, or on the stove using a double boiler set over low heat.
2. Add the Nutella, and vanilla and salt, if using, and stir until well combined.
3. Pour into an 8-inch square pan that has been lined with non-stick tin foil or parchment paper.
4. Spread the fudge into an even layer.
5. Cover and let sit at room temperature for 3-4 hours or refrigerate for about an hour until firm.
6. If chilled, allow the fudge to warm up to room temperature for about 60 minutes.
7. Remove fudge from pan, peel off the tin foil or parchment paper, and cut into 36 squares.

NOTES

To make a double boiler fill a pan with 1 inch of water then set a snug-fitting bowl over top.

buckeye fudge

Serves 25 | Prep 10 mins | Cook 5 mins

INGREDIENTS

Peanut Butter Layer

2 cups creamy peanut butter

4 tablespoons butter

3 tablespoons heavy whipping cream

1/4 teaspoon table salt

2 1/2 cups powdered sugar

Chocolate Ganache Layer

3/4 cup heavy whipping cream

12 ounces dark chocolate.

DIRECTIONS

1. Heat peanut butter, butter, 3 tablespoons heavy whipping cream, and salt in the microwave at high power for 30 second bursts of power, stirring after each until melted.
2. Stir in the powdered sugar until completely blended.
3. Spread into a greased or lined 8-inch square pan.
4. Heat the whipping cream on the stove top set over medium heat just until it comes to a simmer.
5. Pour the hot cream over the chocolate and let rest for 3 minutes before stirring until smooth.
6. Spread over top of the peanut butter fudge layer.
7. Cover and set aside at room temperature for 8 hours until the fudge firms up.
8. Remove the fudge and cut it into 25 pieces.

NOTES

For smooth chocolate ganache do not allow the cream come to a full boil.

cherry cola fudge

Serves 36 | Prep 10 mins | Cook 5 mins

INGREDIENTS

28 oz. white chocolate chips

14 ounces sweetened condensed milk

1 tablespoon maraschino cherry juice

6 drops cherry flavoring

22 maraschino cherries, drained, dried, and quartered

8 oz. semi-sweet chocolate

1 cup sweet condensed milk

8 drops cola flavoring

DIRECTIONS

1. Heat the white chocolate and 1 can sweetened condensed milk in the microwave, for 1 minute, then stir. Heat for 45 seconds, then let rest for 3 minutes.
2. Stir a little then add the maraschino cherry juice, cherry flavoring, and the maraschino cherry pieces.
3. Spread the fudge into a lined 8-inch square pan.
4. Chill in the refrigerator for about 30 minutes.
5. Heat the whipping cream on the stove top set over medium heat just until it comes to a simmer.
6. Pour the hot cream over the chocolate and let rest for 3 minutes before stirring until smooth.
7. Stir in 8 drops of cola flavoring.
8. Spread in an even layer over the cherry fudge.
9. Cover and let rest at room temperature for about 8 hours until firm before cutting into 36 squares.

NOTES

You can find small bottles of candy oils including cola flavoring at craft, grocery, or drug stores.

monster fudge

Serves 25 | Prep 15 mins | Cook 1 1/2 mins

INGREDIENTS

DIRECTIONS

24 ounces (4 cups) light blue candy melts

14 ounces (1 can) sweetened condensed milk

1 cup broken mix of mini chocolate chip cookies and mini chocolate sandwich cookies

1 tablespoon candy eyes

1. Line an 8-inch square baking pan with non-stick foil or lightly-greased parchment paper.
2. Combine the candy melts and sweetened condensed milk in a microwave-safe bowl.
3. Heat at 70% power for 90 seconds. Allow the bowl to rest in the warm microwave for 3 minutes.
4. Stir the chocolate until melted. If needed, heat 15 second increments at 70% power, stirring after each.
5. Pour the fudge evenly in the pan.
6. Top with cookies and candy eyes, gently pressing into the fudge.
7. Allow the fudge to cool at room temperature for about 8 hours or chill in the refrigerator until firm, about 3 hours.
8. Cut into squares.

NOTES

Find candy melts and candy eyes in the craft store or online.

tiger butter fudge

Serves 16 | Prep 10 mins | Cook 5 mins

INGREDIENTS

Peanut Butter Layer

12 ounces white chips or white Candy Melts (see notes)

6 ounces Reese's Peanut Butter Chips

12 ounces Jif Creamy Peanut Butter

pinch of salt

Chocolate Ganache Layer

4 ounces dark chocolate chips

1/4 cup heavy whipping cream

DIRECTIONS

1. Combine white and peanut butter chips and heat for 30 second bursts of high power in the microwave, stirring after each, until melted.
2. Add peanut butter and salt and stir until well combined.
3. Pour into a parchment paper or non-stick tin foil-lined 8-inch square baking pan and set aside.
4. Heat the whipping cream on the stove top set over medium heat just until it comes to a simmer.
5. Pour over the chocolate and let rest for 3 minutes before stirring until smooth.
6. Drizzle the chocolate ganache over top of the fudge.
7. Use a toothpick to swirl the two layers together.
8. Cover and set aside at room temperature for 8 hours until the fudge firms up.
9. Remove the fudge and cut it into 16 pieces.

NOTES

If you use pure white chocolate with cocoa butter listed in the ingredients, add an extra 2 ounces.

cookie dough fudge

Serves 36 | Prep 10 mins | Cook 3 mins

INGREDIENTS

Cookie Dough
1 cup mini chocolate chips
1 cup flour
1/2 cup (1 stick) butter, softened
1/4 cup granulated sugar
1/2 cup light brown sugar
2 tablespoons milk
1 1/2 teaspoons vanilla
1/2 teaspoon salt

Fudge
14 ounces white chocolate
14 ounces sweetened condensed milk

DIRECTIONS

1. Freeze the chocolate chips for 20 minutes.
2. Heat the flour in the microwave for three 30-second bursts of high power, stirring after each, then cool.
3. Beat the butter and both sugars until light and fluffy.
4. Add the vanilla and milk and beat to combine.
5. Stir in the flour and salt.
6. Combine the white chocolate chips and sweetened condensed milk in a large microwave-safe mixing bowl.
7. Heat in the microwave at 70% power for 90 seconds.
8. Let the bowl sit in the microwave for 3 minutes before removing and stirring until melted.
9. Stir the cookie dough into the melted chocolate.
10. Fold in the chilled chocolate chips.
11. Pour the fudge into a greased or lined pan.
12. Chill for at least 3 hours then cut into 36 small squares.

NOTES

You must pasteurize the flour (heat the flour to 160 degrees F) to eliminate the risk of E Coli.

chocolate pretzel fudge

Serves 25 | Prep 10 mins | Cook 1 1/2 mins

INGREDIENTS

16 ounces (2 ⅔ cups) semi-sweet chocolate chips

14 ounces (1 can) sweetened condensed milk

20 to 30 mini pretzels

3 pinches coarse salt

DIRECTIONS

1. Line an 8 or 9-inch square baking pan with non-stick foil or lightly-greased parchment paper.
2. Combine the chocolate and sweetened condensed milk in a microwave-safe bowl.
3. Heat at 70% power for 90 seconds. Allow the bowl to rest in the warm microwave for 3 minutes.
4. Stir the chocolate until melted. If needed, heat 15 second increments at 70% power, stirring after each.
5. Pour the fudge evenly in the pan. Gently press the pretzels on the top of the fudge. You should fit 4 to 5 across and 5 down in an 8-inch pan.
6. Allow the fudge to cool at room temperature for about 8 hours or chill in the refrigerator until firm, about 3 hours.
7. Cut into squares so each pretzel remains whole.

NOTES

Check out Fudge Basics for instructions to prepare this fudge on the stove-top!

s'mores fudge

Serves 36 | Prep 10 mins | Cook 1 1/2 mins

INGREDIENTS

1 cup mini marshmallows

12 ounces semi-sweet chocolate, finely chopped bars or chips

14 ounces sweetened condensed milk

3 graham crackers, broken into small pieces

DIRECTIONS

1. Spread the marshmallows a silicone mat lined pan.
2. Broil on the top rack in the oven until browned.
3. Cool then freeze the marshmallows for 10 minutes.
4. Stir together the chocolate chips and sweetened condensed milk in a microwave-safe mixing bowl.
5. Heat in the microwave at 70% power for 90 seconds.
6. Let the bowl sit in the microwave for 3 minutes.
7. Remove and stir until the chocolate melts.
8. If needed, heat for an additional 15-seconds.
9. Stir in about ¾ of the graham crackers & marshmallows.
10. Spread the fudge into a greased or lined 8-inch square pan then sprinkle the remaining graham cracker pieces and marshmallows over top.
11. Cover and refrigerate for 3-4 hours until firm.
12. Remove fudge from pan and cut into 36 squares.

NOTES

If you don't have a silicone mat then, line your baking pan with tin foil sprayed with non-stick spray.

red velvet fudge

Serves 36 | Prep 10 mins | Cook 1 1/2 mins

INGREDIENTS

Red Velvet Fudge Layer

16 ounces milk chocolate

14 ounces sweetened condensed milk

1 pinch salt

3/4 teaspoon red food coloring

Cream Cheese Frosting

2 ounces cream cheese

1 tablespoon salted butter

3.5 ounces sifted powdered sugar (1 cup)

1/4 teaspoon vanilla extract

2 oz. white chocolate, melted

DIRECTIONS

1. Stir together the milk chocolate and sweetened condensed milk.
2. Heat in the microwave at 70% power for 90 seconds.
3. Let rest in the microwave for 3 minutes, then stir.
4. Add salt and red food coloring and continue stirring until all the chocolate melts.
5. Pour the fudge into a greased or lined 8-inch pan.
6. Using an electric mixer, beat the cream cheese and butter until light and fluffy.
7. Add the powdered sugar and vanilla and beat to combine.
8. Beat in the melted white chocolate. (see notes)
9. Spread over the milk chocolate fudge layer.
10. Cover and chill for 3-4 hours until firm.
11. Remove from the pan and cut into 36 squares.

NOTES

If the frosting becomes lumpy, heat in the microwave for 10 seconds then stir until creamy.

cotton candy fudge

Serves 16 | Prep 10 mins | Cook 1 1/2 mins

INGREDIENTS

18-21 oz. white chocolate chips

14 ounces sweetened condensed milk

1 teaspoon cotton candy flavoring

food coloring: pink, blue, white

*If using pure white chocolate, with cocoa butter use 21 ounces of white chocolate otherwise use 18 ounces.

NOTES

The white coloring lightens the cream colored white chocolate chips so the pink & blue are vibrant.

DIRECTIONS

1. Stir the white chocolate and sweetened condensed milk and heat at 70% power for 90 seconds.
2. Let the bowl rest in the microwave for 3 minutes before stirring until smooth.
3. If needed heat for an additional 10-15 seconds.
4. Stir in the cotton candy flavoring and a few drops of white food coloring.
5. Spoon about 3 tablespoons of the warm fudge into a small bowl and color that using blue coloring and spoon into a pastry bag or zip-top bag.
6. Color the remaining fudge using pink food coloring and spread it into a greased or lined 8-inch square pan.
7. Pipe 16 swirls of blue fudge onto the pink fudge.
8. Cover and chill for 3-4 hours until firm.
9. Remove from pan and cut into 16 squares.

boozy fudge

whiskey fudge

Serves 25 | Prep 10 mins | Cook 1 1/2 mins

INGREDIENTS

1 pound confectioner's (powdered) sugar

1/2 cup whiskey

9 ounces (1 1/2 cups) semi-sweet chocolate chips

DIRECTIONS

1. Line an 8 or 9-inch baking pan with non-stick foil or lightly-greased parchment paper.
2. Whisk together the confectioner's sugar and liquor in a large bowl. It will look like icing.
3. Place the chocolate chips in a microwave-safe bowl.
4. Heat at 70% power for 90 seconds. Allow the bowl to rest in the warm microwave for 3 minutes.
5. Stir the chocolate until melted and smooth. If needed, microwave at additional 15 second intervals.
6. Scrape the chocolate into the alcohol mixture and stir until very smooth.
7. Pour the mixture into the baking pan.
8. Allow the fudge to cool at room temperature for about 8 hours or chill in the refrigerator until firm, about 3 hours.
9. Cut into 25 squares.

NOTES

Be sure to use room-temperature alcohol so your chocolate doesn't seize!

Irish creme fudge

Serves 25 | Prep 10 mins | Cook 1 1/2 mins

INGREDIENTS

1 pound confectioner's (powdered) sugar

3/4 cup Irish creme liqueur

9 ounces (1 1/2 cups) semi-sweet chocolate chips

2 to 3 pinches coarse sea salt (optional)

DIRECTIONS

1. Line an 8 or 9-inch baking pan with non-stick foil or lightly-greased parchment paper.
2. Whisk together the confectioner's sugar and liquor in a large bowl. It will look like icing.
3. Place the chocolate chips in a microwave-safe bowl.
4. Heat at 70% power for 90 seconds. Allow the bowl to rest in the warm microwave for 3 minutes.
5. Stir the chocolate until melted and smooth. If needed, microwave at additional 15 second intervals.
6. Scrape the chocolate into the alcohol mixture and stir until very smooth.
7. Pour the mixture into the baking pan.
8. If using, sprinkle salt on top.
9. Allow the fudge to cool at room temperature for about 8 hours or chill in the refrigerator until firm, about 3 hours.
10. Cut into 25 squares.

NOTES

Be sure to use room-temperature alcohol so your chocolate doesn't seize!

vodka fudge

Serves 25 | Prep 10 mins | Cook 1 1/2 mins

INGREDIENTS

DIRECTIONS

1 pound confectioner's (powdered) sugar

1/2 cup vodka

9 ounces (1 1/2 cups) semi-sweet chocolate chips

1. Line an 8 or 9-inch baking pan with non-stick foil or lightly-greased parchment paper.
2. Whisk together the confectioner's sugar and vodka in a large bowl. It will look like icing.
3. Place the chocolate chips in a microwave-safe bowl.
4. Heat at 70% power for 90 seconds. Allow the bowl to rest in the warm microwave for 3 minutes.
5. Stir the chocolate until melted and smooth. If needed, microwave at additional 15 second intervals.
6. Scrape the chocolate into the alcohol mixture and stir until very smooth.
7. Pour the mixture into the baking pan.
8. Allow the fudge to cool at room temperature for about 8 hours or chill in the refrigerator until firm, about 3 hours.
9. Cut into 25 squares.

NOTES
Be sure to use room-temperature alcohol so your chocolate doesn't seize!

cinnamon whiskey fudge

Serves 60 | Prep 10 mins | Cook 1 1/2 mins

INGREDIENTS

2 pounds confectioner's (powdered) sugar

1 cup cinnamon whiskey

12 ounces (2 cups) semi-sweet chocolate chips

cinnamon candies (optional)

DIRECTIONS

1. Line an 9 x 13-inch baking pan with non-stick foil or lightly-greased parchment paper.
2. Whisk together the confectioner's sugar and whiskey in a large bowl. It will look like icing.
3. Place the chocolate chips in a microwave-safe bowl.
4. Heat at 70% power for 90 seconds. Allow the bowl to rest in the warm microwave for 3 minutes.
5. Stir the chocolate until melted and smooth. If needed, microwave at additional 15 second intervals.
6. Scrape the chocolate into the alcohol mixture and stir until very smooth.
7. Pour the mixture into the baking pan.
8. Sprinkle candies on top, if using.
9. Allow the fudge to cool at room temperature for about 8 hours or chill in the refrigerator until firm, about 3 hours.
10. Cut into squares.

NOTES

Be sure to use room-temperature alcohol so your chocolate doesn't seize!

gin fudge

Serves 60 | Prep 15 mins | Cook 1 1/2 mins

INGREDIENTS

DIRECTIONS

2 pounds confectioner's (powdered) sugar

1 cup gin

12 ounces (2 cups) white chocolate chips

zest of 2 limes, optional

1. Line 9 x 13-inch baking pan with non-stick foil or lightly-greased parchment paper.
2. Whisk together the confectioner's sugar and gin in a large bowl. It will look like icing.
3. Place the chocolate chips in a microwave-safe bowl.
4. Heat at 70% power for 90 seconds. Allow the bowl to rest in the warm microwave for 3 minutes.
5. Stir the chocolate until melted and smooth. If needed, microwave at additional 15 second intervals.
6. Scrape the chocolate into the alcohol mixture and stir until very smooth.
7. Pour the mixture into the baking pan.
8. Sprinkle lime zest on top, if using.
9. Allow the fudge to cool at room temperature for about 8 hours or chill in the refrigerator until firm, about 3 hours.
10. Cut into squares.

NOTES

Be sure to use room-temperature alcohol so your chocolate doesn't seize!

tequila fudge

Serves 60 | Prep 15 mins | Cook 1 1/2 mins

INGREDIENTS

2 pounds confectioner's (powdered) sugar

1 cup tequila

12 ounces (2 cups) semi-sweet chocolate chips

zest of 2 limes, optional

DIRECTIONS

1. Line 9 x 13-inch baking pan with non-stick foil or lightly-greased parchment paper.
2. Whisk together the confectioner's sugar and tequila in a large bowl. It will look like icing.
3. Place the chocolate chips in a microwave-safe bowl.
4. Heat at 70% power for 90 seconds. Allow the bowl to rest in the warm microwave for 3 minutes.
5. Stir the chocolate until melted and smooth. If needed, microwave at additional 15 second intervals.
6. Scrape the chocolate into the alcohol mixture and stir until very smooth.
7. Pour the mixture into the baking pan.
8. Sprinkle lime zest on top, if using.
9. Allow the fudge to cool at room temperature for about 8 hours or chill in the refrigerator until firm, about 3 hours.
10. Cut into squares.

NOTES

Be sure to use room-temperature alcohol so your chocolate doesn't seize!

rum fudge

Serves 60 | Prep 15 mins | Cook 1 1/2 mins

INGREDIENTS

2 pounds confectioner's (powdered) sugar

1 cup rum

12 ounces (2 cups) semi-sweet chocolate chips

½ cup shredded coconut, optional

DIRECTIONS

1. Line 9 x 13-inch baking pan with non-stick foil or lightly-greased parchment paper.
2. Whisk together the confectioner's sugar and rum in a large bowl. It will look like icing.
3. Place the chocolate chips in a microwave-safe bowl.
4. Heat at 70% power for 90 seconds. Allow the bowl to rest in the warm microwave for 3 minutes.
5. Stir the chocolate until melted and smooth. If needed, microwave at additional 15 second intervals.
6. Scrape the chocolate into the alcohol mixture and stir until very smooth.
7. Pour the mixture into the baking pan.
8. Sprinkle coconut on top, if using.
9. Allow the fudge to cool at room temperature for about 8 hours or chill in the refrigerator until firm, about 3 hours.
10. Cut into squares.

NOTES

Be sure to use room-temperature alcohol so your chocolate doesn't seize!

index

Baking Pan, 1
Boozy Fudge, 63
Buckeye Fudge, 54
Butter Pecan Fudge, 21
Butterscotch Fudge, 16
Cake Batter Funfetti Fudge, 53
Caramel Fudge, 48
Cherry Cola Fudge, 55
Chocolate Cashew Butter Fudge, 22
Chocolate Coconut Fudge, 17
Chocolate Hazelnut Spread Fudge, 49
Chocolate Peanut Butter Fudge, 9
Chocolate Peanut Butter Cup Fudge, 51
Chocolate Peppermint Fudge, 42
Chocolate Pretzel Fudge, 59
Chocolate, Types, 3
- Butterscotch Chips, 3
- Milk Chocolate, 3
- Peanut Butter Chips, 3
- Pure Dark Chocolate, 3
- Pure White Chocolate, 3
- Salted Caramel Chips, 3

Christmas Fudge, 39, 40, 41, 42, 43, 44, 45, 46
Cinnamon Whiskey Fudge, 67
Cookies and Cream Fudge, 15
Cookie Butter Fudge, 52
Cookie Dough Fudge, 58
Creamsicle Fudge, 27
Cotton Candy Fudge, 62
Dark Chocolate Fudge, 7
Dark Chocolate Raspberry Fudge, 29
Double Boiler, 2
Dry Fudge, 5
Easter Orange Fudge Carrots, 35
Easy Christmas Fudge, 45
Eggnog Fudge, 41
Frosting, 2
Frosting Fudge, 13
Fruit curd, 2
Fudge Basics, 1
Fudge Hearts, 32
Gin Fudge, 68
Greasy Fudge, 5
Halloween Fudge, 37
Holiday Fudge, 30
Independence Day Fudge, 36

Irish Crème Fudge, 65
Jam, 2
Key Lime Fudge, 28
Lemon Fudge, 25
Maple Fudge, 18
Maple Walnut Fudge, 23
Marshmallow Fudge, 14
Mermaid Fudge, 50
Microwave, 2
Milk Chocolate Fudge, 11
Milk Chocolate Fudge Turkeys, 38
Mint Chocolate Chip Fudge, 12
Monster Fudge, 56
New Year's Eve Countdown Clock Fudge, 31
New Year's Eve Fudge, 31
Nut butter, 2
Nutty and Fruity Fudge, 19
"Oh Fudge!" Soap Fudge, 46
Peanut Blossom Fudge, 39
Peanut Butter Fudge, 8
Peppermint Bark Fudge, 40
Pumpkin Fudge, 24
Rainbow Fudge, 34
Red Velvet Fudge, 61
Red, White, and Blue Fudge, 36
Reindeer Fudge, 44
Rocky Road Fudge, 20
Rum Fudge, 70
S'mores Fudge, 60
Snowmen Fudge, 43
Soft Fudge, 5
Store Fudge, 4
Stove-top, 2
St. Patrick's Day Fudge, 34, 65
Strawberry Frosting Fudge, 33
Strawberry Fudge, 29
Sweetened Condensed Milk, 2
Tequila Fudge, 69
Tiger Butter Fudge, 57
Thanksgiving Fudge, 24, 38
Traditional Fudge, 6
Unconventional Fudge, 47
Valentine's Day Fudge, 32, 33, 61
Vanilla Fudge, 10
Vodka Fudge, 66
Whiskey Fudge, 64
Zombie Fudge, 37

Printed in Great Britain
by Amazon